Richard Watson Gilder, America Project Making of

A New Day

A Poem in Songs and Sonnets

Richard Watson Gilder, America Project Making of

A New Day
A Poem in Songs and Sonnets

ISBN/EAN: 9783744709255

Printed in Europe, USA, Canada, Australia, Japan

Cover: Foto ©Thomas Meinert / pixelio.de

More available books at **www.hansebooks.com**

THE NEW DAY

A POEM IN SONGS AND SONNETS

BY

RICHARD WATSON GILDER

NEW YORK

SCRIBNER, ARMSTRONG, AND COMPANY

1876

PRELUDE.

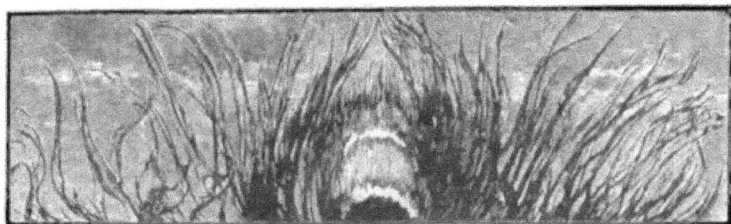

THE night was dark, though sometimes a faint
    star
A little while a little space made bright.
The night was long and like an iron bar
Lay heavy on the land : till o'er the sea
Slowly, within the East, there grew a light
Which half was starlight, and half seemed to be
The herald of a greater.   The pale white
Turned slowly to pale rose, and up the height
Of heaven slowly climbed.   The gray sea grew
Rose-colored like the sky.   A white gull flew
Straight toward the utmost boundary of the East
Where slowly the rose gathered and increased.
It was as on the opening of a door
By one that in his hand a lamp doth hold,
Whose flame is hidden by the garment's fold —
The still air moves, the wide room is less dim.

More bright the East became, the ocean turned
Dark and more dark against the brightening sky —
Sharper against the sky the long sea line.
The hollows of the breakers on the shore
Were green like leaves whereon no sun doth shine,
Though white the outer branches of the tree.
From rose to red the level heaven burned ;
Then sudden, as if a sword fell from on high,
A blade of gold flashed on the horizon's rim.

PART I.

I.

AFTER THE ITALIAN.

I KNOW not if I love her overmuch ;
But this I know, that when unto her face
She lifts her hand, which rests there, still, a space,
Then slowly falls — 'tis I who feel that touch.
And when she sudden shakes her head, with such
A look, I soon her secret meaning trace.
So when she runs I think 'tis I who race.
Like a poor cripple who has lost his crutch
I am if she is gone ; and when she goes,
I know not why, for that is a strange art —
As if myself should from myself depart.
I know not if I love her more than those
Her lovers, but I know for that red rosé
She covers in her hair, I 'd give my heart.

II.

A RIDDLE OF LOVERS.

I.

THERE lived a lady who was lovelier
   Than anything that my poor skill may paint,
   Though I would follow round the world till faint
I fell, for just one little look at her.
Who said she seemed like this or that did err ;
   Like her dear self she was, alone, — no taint
   From touch of mortal or of earth, — blest saint
Serene, with many a faithful worshipper !
There is no poet's poesy would not
   When laid against the whiteness of her meek,
Proud, solemn face make there a pitiful blot :
   It is so strange that I can never speak
Of her without a tear ; — oh, I forgot !
   This surely may fall blameless on her cheek.

II.

But of my lady's lovers there were two
  Who loved her more than all ; nor she nor they
  Guessed which of these loved better, for one way
This had of loving, that another knew.
One round her neck brave arms of empire threw
  And covered her with kisses where she lay.
  The other sat apart, nor did betray
Sweet sorrow at that sight ; but rather drew
His pleasure of his lady through the soul
  And sense of this one.   So there truly ran
Two separate loves through one embrace ; the whole
  This lady had of both, when one began
To clasp her close and win her to love's goal.
  Now read my lovers' riddle if you can !

III.

"A DUN, BLEAK STRETCH THAT SLANTS TO THE SALT SEA'S GRAY."

A DUN, bleak stretch that slants to the salt sea's gray —
　　Rock-strewn, and scarred by fire, and rough with
　　　　stubble, —
With here and there a bold, bright touch of color —
Berries and yellow leaves — that make the dolor
　　More dolorous still.　Above, a sky of trouble.

But now a light is lifted in the air ;
　　And though the sky is shadowed, fold on fold,
　　By clouds that have the lightnings in their hold,
That western gleam makes all the dim earth fair —
　　The sun shines forth and the gray sea is gold.

IV.

LOVE IN WONDER.

I saw a picture of a lover wan,
  Who stepping from dark wood doth thrust apart
  Strong-matted, thorny branches, whose keen smart
He heeds in nowise, if he only can
Win the red rose his lady, like a fan,
  Holds daintily.   She, listening to her heart,
  Doth look another way. Now would she start,
And weep, and suffer sorrow, if he ran —
For utter love of her — swift, sobbing, back
  Into those terrible shadows, terribler
Because her whiteness made their black more black !
  A little while he waits, lest he should err ;
A while he wonders, secretly. — Alack !
  He could so gladly die, or live for her.

V.

LOVE GROWN BOLD.

THIS is her picture painted ere mine eyes
   Her ever holy face had looked upon.
   She sitteth in a silence of her own ;
Behind her, on the ground, a red rose lies :
Her thinking brow is bent, nor doth arise
   Her gaze from that shut book whose word unknown
   Her firm hands hide from her ; — there all alone
She sitteth in thought-trouble, maidenwise.
And now her lover waiting wondereth
   Whether the joy of all joys draweth near :
Shall his brave fingers like a tender breath
   That shut book open for her, wide and clear ?
From him who her sweet shadow worshippeth
   Now will she take the rose, and hold it dear ?

INTERLUDE.

THE sun rose swift and sent a golden gleam
   Across the moving waters to the land ;
Then for a certain while it seemed to stand
In a clear place, midway 'twixt sea and cloud ;
Whence rising swift again it passed behind
Full many a long and narrow cloud-wrought beam
Encased in gold unearthly, that was mined
From out the hollow caverns of the wind.
These first revealed its face and next did shroud,
While still the daylight grew, and joy thereby
Lit all the windy stretches of the sky :

Until a shadow darkened from the east
And sprang upon the ocean like a beast.

PART II.

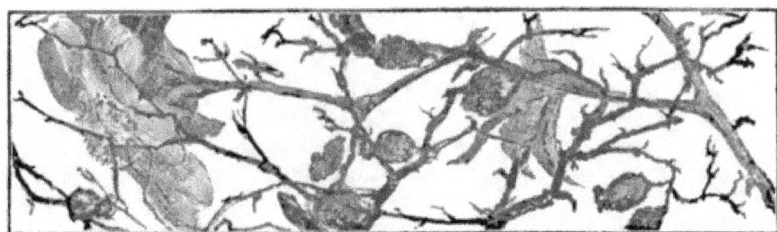

THERE was a field green and fragrant with grass and flowers, and flooded with light from the sun, and the air of it throbbed with the songs of birds. It was yet morning when a great darkness came, and fire followed lightning over the face of it, and the singing birds fell dead upon the blackened grass. The thunder and the flame passed, but it was still dark, — till a ray of light touched the field's edge and grew, little by little. Then one who listened heard — not the song of birds again, but the flutter of broken wings.

II.

THE DARK ROOM.

I.

A MAIDEN sought her love in a dark room, —
  So early had she yearned from yearning sleep,
  So hard it was from her true love to keep, —
And blind she went through that all-silent gloom,
Like one who wanders weeping in a tomb.
  Heavy her heart, but her light fingers leap
  With restless grasp and question in that deep
Unanswering void.   Now when a hand did loom
  At last, how swift her warm impassioned face
Pressed 'gainst the black and solemn-yielding air, ·
  As near more near she groped to that bright place.
And seized the hand, and drowned it with her hair,
  And bent her body to his fierce embrace,
And was so joyful in the darkness there.

II.

GREAT GOD ! the arms wherein that maiden fell
　Were not her lover's ; I am her lover — I,
　Who sat here in the shadows silently —
Silent with gladness, for I thought, O hell !
I thought to me she moved, and all was well.
　She saw me not yet dimly could descry
　That beautiful hand of his and with a sigh
Sank on his treacherous, damned breast.　The spell
Of the Evil One was on me.　All in vain
　I strove to speak — my parched lips were dumb.
See ! see ! the wan and whitening window-pane !
　See, in the night, the awful morning bloom !
Too late she will know all !　God I send thy rain
　Of death, nor let the sun of waking come !

III.

"YEA, COME TO ME YE SUFFERING!"

YEA, come to me ye suffering! To all
  I am a brother now! 'T was not in vain
  I saw our Sorrowful Sister's face, who slain
Yet lives; whose voice when she doth weep and call
Is silent. When she weeps? Nay, nay! the pall
  Is on her tears too — they are dead. The rain
  Is molten-hot dust-dry from her dull pain : —
Like ashes from the burning heavens that fall.
I know the world-wide, lovely, living lie ;
  I know the truth that better were unknown.
I know the joyful laugh that is a cry
    Torn from a heart whence hope and faith have
      flown,
And yet beats on, and will not, dare not die.
  I know the anguish without word or moan.

IV.

"I MET A TRAVELLER ON THE ROAD."

I MET a traveller on the road,
His face was wrinkled, wan, and sad ;
His back was bent beneath a load
Too big for one whose sinews had
Been wrenched by labor overmuch :
Or was he withered in the clutch
Of his strong soul gone sanely mad !
His face was wan, his feet were weary,
Yet he unresting went with such
A strange, still, patient mien ; a look
Set forward in the empty air,
As he were reading an unseen book.
His awful, fixed smile did tear
My soul with pity.   I could bear
That better than what next I knew
When, sorrow-drawn, I came more near ;
For suddenly I seemed to hear

The broken echo of a song
Sung in the sunlight, far away.
His lips were parted, but unmoved
By words. He sang as dreamers do,
And not as if he heard and loved
The thing he sang. It was not sad —
But, O my God, that memory blot!
The livelong night, the livelong day,
It comes and will not be forgot —
That traveller's song, serene and cheery!
He stood beside the level brook —
Nor drank the water, nor bathed his brow,
Nor from his back the burden shook.
He stood, and yet he did not rest;
His hand lay dead on his dead breast;
His eyes climbed up in aimless quest,
Then close did to that mirror bow —
And looking down I saw in place
Of his, my own wan, wrinkled face!

V.

WRITTEN ON A FLY-LEAF OF "SHAKE-SPEARE'S SONNETS."

WHEN will true love be love without alloy :
  Shine greatly free from sinful circumstance !
  When will the canker of unheavenly chance
Eat not the bud of that most heavenly joy !
When will true love meet love not as a coy
  Retreating light that leads a deathful dance,
  But as a firm fixed fire that doth enhance
The beauty of all beauty !   Will the employ
Of poets ever be too well to show
  That mightiest love with sharpest pain doth writhe ;
  That underneath the fair, caressing glove
Hides evermore the iron hand ; and though
  Love's flower alone is good, if we would prove
  Its perfect bloom, our breath slays like a scythe !

·

VI.

"AND WERE THAT BEST!"

AND were that best, Love, dreamless, endless sleep !
  Gone all the fervor of the mortal day ;
  The daylight gone, and gone the starry ray !
And were that best, Love, rest serene and deep !
Gone labor and desire ; no arduous steep
  To climb, no songs to sing, no prayers to pray,
  No help for those who perish by the way,
No laughter 'midst our tears, no tears to weep !
And were that best, Love, sleep with no sweet dream,
  Nor memory of any thing in life —
    Stark death that neither help nor hurt can know !
Oh, rather, Love, the sorrow-bringing gleam,
  The living day's long agony and strife !
    Rather strong love in pain — the waking woe !

VII.

"THERE IS NOTHING NEW UNDER THE SUN."

THERE is nothing new under the sun ;
　　There is no new hope or despair ;
The agony just begun
　　Is as old as the earth and the air.
My secret soul of bliss
　　Is one with the singing star's,
And the ancient mountains miss
　　No hurt that my being mars.

I know as I know my life,
　　I know as I know my pain,
That there is no lonely strife,
　　That he is mad who would gain
A separate balm for his woe,
　　A single pity and cover :
The one great God I know
　　Hears the same prayer over and over.

I know it because at the portal
  Of Heaven I bowed and cried,
And I said, "Was ever a mortal
  Thus crowned and crucified !
My praise thou hast made my blame ;
  My best thou hast made my worst ;
My good thou hast turned to shame ;
  My drink is a flaming thirst."

But scarce my prayer was said
  Ere from that place I turned ;
I trembled, I hung my head,
  My cheek, shame-litten, burned :
For there where I bowed down
  In my boastful agony,
I thought of thy cross and crown, —
  O Christ ! I remembered thee.

'

VIII.

LOVE'S CRUELTY.

" AND this then is thy love," I hear thee say,
　" Now spare me, if thou lov'st me, this last woe ! "
　O Love, Love, Love ! gladly would I do so ;
But I am not my own ; I must obey
My Lord ; I am LOVE'S slave : his sway
　Is cruel as the grave.　When he says, Lo !
　I bid thee come ; I come.　When he says, Go !
I go.　When he says, Slay ; I needs must slay.
As cruel as the grave?　Yea, crueller.
　Cruel as light that pours its stinging flood
Across the dark, and makes an anguished stir
　Of life.　Cruel as life that sends through blood
Of mortal, the immortal pang and spur.
　Cruel as thy remorseless maidenhood.

3

INTERLUDE.

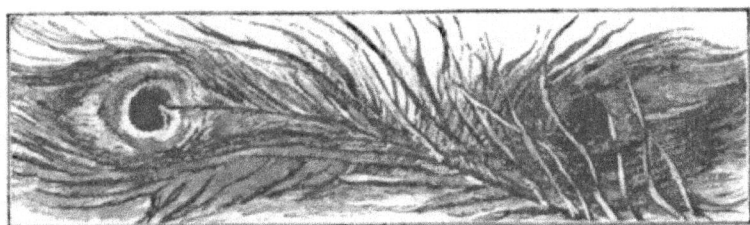

THE cloud was thick that hid the sun from sight
And over all a sombre roof outspread,
Making the day dim with another night —
Not dark like that which passed, but oh! more dread,
For all the glory that had gone before
And all the promise of what yet should be.
Like snow at night the wind-blown hills of sand
Shone with an inward light far down the land:
Beneath the lowering sky black was the sea
Across whose waves a bird came flying low —
Swift on the wind with wing-beat halt and slow —
From out the dull east toward the foamy shore.
There was an awful waiting in the earth
As if a mystery greatened to its birth:
Though late it seemed, the day was just begun
When lo! at last, the many-colored bow
Stood in the heavens over against the sun.

PART III.

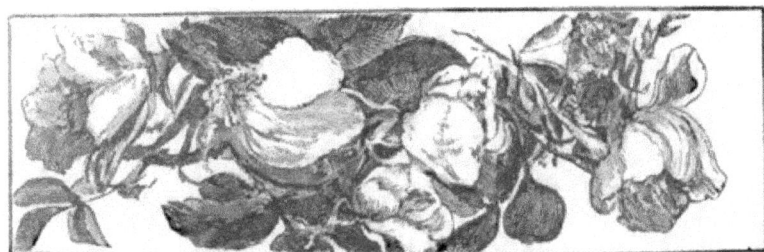

I.

"THE PALLID WATCHER OF THE EAST-ERN SKIES."

THE pallid watcher of the eastern skies
   Who through the suffering night did wait forlorn,
  When comes the first faint purple of the morn
Waiteth no longer. To his happy eyes
The promised near the promise following flies,
   Nor is his soul with sullen anguish torn,
   Nor curseth he the day when he was born.
From the damp ground he doth awondering rise,
Firm set his face against the gathering glory, —
   To be so sure that this at last is this,
And not the ancient, bitter-lying story.
   Now he doth pray for strength to bear the bliss,
While, bending o'er the mountain red and hoary,
   The morning crowns him with a golden kiss.

II.

"I WILL BE BRAVE FOR THEE."

I WILL be brave for thee, dear heart ; for thee
　My boasted bravery forego.　I will
　For thee be wise as that wise king, until
That wise king's fool for thy sake I may be.
No grievous cost in anything I see
　That brings thee bliss, or only keeps thee, still,
　In painless peace.　So Heaven but thy cup fill,
Be empty mine unto eternity !
Come to me, Love, and let me touch thy face !
　Lean to me, Love, and breathe on me thy breath !
Fly from me, Love, to some far hiding-place,
　If thy one thought of me or hindereth
Or hurteth thy sweet soul — then grant me grace
　To be forgotten, though that grace be death !

III.

"LOVE ME NOT, LOVE, FOR THAT I FIRST LOVED THEE."

Love me not, Love, for that I first loved thee,
  Nor love me, Love, for thy sweet pity's sake,
  In knowledge of the mortal pain and ache
Which is the fruit of love's blood-veined tree.
Let others for my love give love to me :
  From other souls oh, gladly will I take,
  This heart-dry hunger-thirst of love to slake,
What seas of human pity there may be.
Nay, nay, I care no more how love may grow,
  So that I hear thee answer to my call !
Love me because my piteous tears do flow,
  Or that my love for thee did first befall.
Love me or late or early, fast or slow :
  But love me, Love, for love is one and all !

IV.

BODY AND SOUL.

I.

O THOU my Love, love first my lonely soul!
  Then will this too unworthy body of mine
  Be loved by right and accident divine.
Forget the flesh, that the pure spirit's goal
May be the spirit; let that stand the whole
  Of the thing thou lov'st in me.   So will the shine
  Of sharp soul striking soul make fair and fine
This earthy tenement.   Thou shalt extol
The inner, that the outer lovelier seem.
  Remember well that thy true love doth fear
No deadlier foe than the impassioned dream
  Would   drive   thee   to   him, and   would   hold   thee
      near —
Near to the body, not the soul of him.
  Love first my soul and then both will be dear.

II.

But, Love, for me thy body was the first.
  One day I wandered idly through the town,
  Then entered a cathedral's silence brown
Which sudden thrilled with a strange heavenly burst
Of light and music.   That dazed traveller durst
  Do nothing now but worship and fall down.
  He thought to rest, as did the tired clown
Who sank in longed-for sleep, but there immersed
Found restless vision on vision of beauty rare.
  Moved by thy body's outer majesty
    I entered in thy silent, sacred shrine :
Twas then, all suddenly and unaware,
  Thou didst reveal, O maiden Love ! to me,
    That beautiful singing holy soul of thine.

V.

"THY LOVER, LOVE, WOULD HAVE SOME NOBLER WAY."

THY lover, Love, would have some nobler way
    To tell his love, his noble love to tell,
    Than in these rhymes that ring like silver bell.
Oh, he would lead an army, great and gay,
From conquering to conquer, day by day;
    And when the walls of a proud citadel
    At summons of his guns loud echoing fell, —
That thunder to his Love should murmuring say :
Thee only do I love, dear Love of mine !
    And while men cried : Behold how brave a fight !
        She should read well, oh well, each new emprise :
        This to her lips, this to my lady's eyes !
And though the world were conquered, line on line,
    Still would his love be speechless, day and night.

VI.

"MY LOVE FOR THEE DOTH MARCH LIKE ARMED MEN."

My love for thee doth march like armed men
   Against a queenly city they would take.
   Along that army's front the banners shake ;
Across the mountain and the sun-smit plain
It steadfast sweeps as sweeps the steadfast rain ;
   And now the trumpet makes the still air quake,
   And now the thundering cannon doth awake
Echo on echo, echoing again.
But, lo! the conquest higher than bard had sung :
   Instead of answering cannon comes a small
White flag ; the iron gates are open flung,
   And flowers along the invaders' pathway fall.
The city's conquerors feast their foes among,
   And their brave flags are trophies on her wall.

VII.

AT THE PLAY.

(SALVINI.)

I SAW Othello crouch across the stage
  With quick, hot breaths, arched neck, and eyes all
    white,
  And fingers curved to claws before my sight ;
I heard his sob and scream of brutal rage,
When, like a tiger leaping from a ledge
  Upon his prey, quick as a flash of light
  He leaped on Iago : then in shivering fright
I saw him cower, as against the cage
A tiger springs, then cowers tremulous.
  So sits my soul apart, — as I do here,
    Beholding Shakespeare's thought before me
      move, —
Calm doth my soul behold my passion thus
  Beat vainly 'gainst expression. Voice nor tear
    Can tell the wild, great agony of my love.

VIII.

"WHAT WOULD I SAVE THEE FROM?"

WHAT would I save thee from, dear heart, dear heart?
  Not from what Heaven may send thee of its pain ;
  Not from fierce sunshine or the scathing rain ;
The pang of pleasure ; passion's wound and smart ;
Not from the long glad agony of thine art ;
  Nor loss of faithful friend, nor any gain
  Of growth by grief.   I would not thee restrain
From needful death.   But O, thou other part
Of me ! — through whom the whole world I behold,
  As through the blue I see the stars above !
In whom the world I find, hid fold on fold !
  Thee would I save from this — nay, do not move !
Fear not, it may not flash, the air is cold ;
  Save thee from this — the lightning of my love.

4

IX.

"WHAT WOULD I WIN THEE TO?'

WHAT would I win thee to? dear heart and true!
　A thought of bliss, a thornless life?　Oh no!
　Through weeping pain, Love, I would let thee go ;
Through　weary　days,　and　widowed　nights ; yea,
　　　through
The Valley of the Shadow, without rue,
　If thou couldst gain the goal, Love, even so.
　I would not win thee to a fruitful woe ;
To best of earth, or best beyond the blue.
And most of all, would thy true lover scorn
　To win thee to himself.　Thou shalt be free
To have or hate !　But O, my golden morn !
　Behold thy lover's passionate bravery —
Mighty, unresting, steadfast, heaven-born —
　To win thee to the light, which is — to thee !

X.

LOVE'S JEALOUSY.

OF other men I know no jealousy,
　　Nor of the maid who holds thee close, oh close :
　　But of the June-red, summer-scented rose,
And of the orange-streaked sunset sky
That wins the soul of thee through thy deep eye ;
　　And of the breeze by thee beloved, that goes
　　O'er thy dear hair and brow ; the song that flows
Into thy heart of hearts, where it may die.
I would I were one moment that sweet show
　　Of flower ; or breeze beloved that toucheth all ;
　　　Or sky that through the summer eve doth burn.
I would I were the song thou lovest so,
　　At sound of me to have thine eyelid fall :
　　　But I would then to something human turn.

XI.

LOVE'S MONOTONE.

Thou art so used, Love, to thine own bird's song, —
  Sung to thine ear in love's low monotone,
  Sung to thee only, Love, to thee alone
Of all the listening world, — that I among
My doubts find this the leader of the throng :
  Haply the music hath accustomed grown
  And no more music is to thee ; my own
Too faithful argument works its own wrong.
I have no art of silence, Love ; I sing
  Because my soul is joyful in thy light,
And I cannot refuse thee any thing.
  But should thy bird at last fall silent quite,
Wouldst thou then be a little sorrowing ?
  Think not of me but of thyself to-night.

XIV.

"ONCE WHEN WE WALKED WITHIN A SUMMER FIELD."

ONCE when we walked within a summer field
   I plucked the flower of immortality,
   And said, " Dear Love of mine, I give to thee
This flower of flowers of all the round year's yield ! "
'Twas then thou stood'st, and with one hand didst
     shield
   Thy sun-dazed eyes, and, flinging the other free,
   Spurned from thee that white blossom utterly.
But, Love ! the immortal cannot so be killed.
The generations shall behold thee stand
   Against that western glow in grass dew-wet —
Lord of my life, and lady of the land.
   Nor maid nor lover shall the world forget,
Nor that disdainful wafture of thy hand.
   Thou scornful ! sun and flower shall find thee yet.

XV.

SONG.

I LOVE her gentle forehead,
    And I love her tender hair;
I love her cool, white arms,
    And her neck where it is bare.

I love the smell of her garments;
    I love the touch of her hands;
I love the sky above her,
    And the very ground where she stands.

I love her doubting and anguish;
    I love the love she withholds;
I love my love that loveth her,
    And anew her being moulds.

XVI.

MUSIC.

WHEN on that blessed sea
Where billow on billow breaks; where swift waves
    follow
Waves, and hollow calls to hollow;
Where sea-birds swirl and swing,
And winds through torn shrouds shrill and sing;
Where night is night without a shade;
Where thy soul not afraid,
Though all alone unlonely,
Wanders and wavers, wavers wandering : —
On that accursed sea
One moment only,
Forget one moment, Love, thy fierce content;
Back let thy soul be bent —
Think back, dear Love, O Love, think back to me!

XVII.

"A SONG OF THE MAIDEN MORN."

A song of the maiden morn,
A song for my little maid,
Of the silver sunlight born !

But I am afraid, afraid,
When I come my maid may be
Nothing, there, but a shade.

But oh, her shadow is more to me
Than the shadowless light of eternity !

XVIII.

WORDS IN ABSENCE.

I WOULD that my words were as my fingers,
  So that my Love might feel them move
Slowly over her brow, as lingers
  The sunset wind o'er the world of its love.
I would that my words were as the beating
Of her own heart, that keeps repeating
  My name through the livelong day and the night;
And when my Love her lover misses —
  Longs for and loves in the dark and the light —
I would that my words were as my kisses.
I would that my words her life might fill,
  Be to her earth, and air, and skies.
I would that my words were hushed and still —
  Lost in the light of her eyes.

IX.

"THERE WAS JOY IN ALL."

THERE was joy in all, but I might not win it.
  I looked from the window on meadow and wood,
    On fair green grass that the sun made white ;
  Beyond the river the mountain stood, —
    Blue was the mountain, the river was bright :
  I looked on the land and it was not good ;
I loved not the land, for thou wert not in it.

XX.

THISTLE–DOWN.

FLY, thistle-down, fly
From my lips to the lips that I love !
Fly through the clear daylight :
Flee through the shadowy night,
Over the sea and the land,
Quick as the lark,
Through twilight and dark,
Through lightning and thunder ;
Till no longer asunder
We stand ;
For thy touch like the lips of her lover,
Moves her being to mine, —
We are one in a swoon divine !

Fly thistle-down, fly
From my lips to the lips that I love !

XXI.

"O SWEET WILD ROSES THAT BUD AND BLOW."

O SWEET wild roses that bud and blow
Along the way that my Love may go ;
O moss-green rocks that touch her dress,
And grass that her dear face may press ;

O maple tree whose brooding shade
For her a summer tent has made ;
O golden-rod and brave sun-flower
That flame before my maiden's bower ;

O butterfly on whose light wings
The golden summer sunshine clings ;
O birds that flit o'er wheat and wall,
And from cool hollows pipe and call ;

O falling waters whose distant roar
Sounds like the waves upon the shore ;

O winds that down the valley sweep,
And lightnings from the clouds that leap ;

O skies that bend above the hills,
O gentle rains and babbling rills,
O moon and sun that beam and burn —
Keep safe my Love till I return !

XXII.

THE RIVER.

I KNOW thou art not that brown mountain-side,
  Nor the pale mist that lies along the hills
  And with white joy the deepening valley fills ;
Nor yet the solemn river moving wide
Into that valley, where the hills abide
  But whence too soon the joy, on noiseless wheels,
  Shall lingering lift and, as the moonlight steals
From out the heavens, so into the heavens shall glide.
I know thou art not that gray rock that looms
  Above the water, fringed with scarlet vine ;
    Nor flame of burning meadow ; nor the sedge
    That sways and trembles at the river's edge.
But through all these, dear heart, to me there comes
  Some melancholy absent look of thine.

XXIII.

THE LOVER'S LORD AND MASTER.

I PRAY thee, dear, think not alone of me,
  But think sometimes of my great master, LOVE ;
  His faithful slave he is so far above
That for his sake I would forgotten be :
Though well I know that hidden thus from thee
  Not far away my image then might rove,
  And his sweet countenance in thy mind would move
Ever thy soul to gentler charity.
So when thy lover's self leaps from his song,
  Thou him may love not less for his fair Lord.
  . But that thy love for me grow never small,
  (As bow long bent twangs not the arrowed cord,
And he doth lose his star who looks too long,)
    Sometimes, dear heart, think not of me at all.

5

XXIV.

SONG.

My love grew with the growing night, —
And my love dawned with the new daylight.

XXV.

"A NIGHT OF STARS AND DREAMS."

A NIGHT of stars and dreams, of dreams and sleep ;
 A waking into another empty day —
  But not unlovely all, for then I say,
"To-morrow !" Through the hours that light doth
  creep
Higher in the heavens, as down the heavenly steep
 Sinks the slow sun. Another evening gray,
 Made glorious by the morn that comes that way ;
Another night, and then To-day doth leap
Upon the world ! Oh quick the moments fly
 That bring that one, the hand-maiden and queen
Of moments all ! Swift up the shaking sky
 Rushes the sun from out its dolesome den ;
And then the sacred time doth yearn more nigh ;
 A long, brief waiting in the dark — and then !

XXVI.

A BIRTHDAY SONG.

I THOUGHT this day to bring to thee
A flower that grows on the red rose tree.
I searched the branches, — oh, despair !
Of roses every branch was bare.

I thought to sing thee a birthday song
As wild as my love, as deep and strong.
The song took wing like a frightened bird,
And its music my maiden never heard.

But, Love ! the flower and the song divine
One day of the year shall yet be thine ;
And thou shalt be glad when that rose I bring,
And weep for joy at the song I sing.

XXVII.

"WHAT CAN LOVE DO FOR THEE, LOVE?"

WHAT can love do for thee, Love?
Can it make the green fields greener;
Bluer the skies, and bluer
The eyes of the blue-eyed flowers?
Can it make the May-day showers
More warm and sweet; serener
The heavens after the rain?
Can it make the true things truer —
The sunset's radiant splendor
More exquisite and tender —
The sure things more sure?
Can it take the pang from pain?
(O Love! remember the curtain
Of cloud that lifted last night
And showed the silver light
Of a star!) Can it make more certain
The heart of the heart of all —

The good that works at the root —
The singing soul of love
That throbs in flower and fruit,
In man and earth and brute,
In hell, and heaven above ?
Can its low voice musical
Make dear the day and the night ?

XXVIII.

FRANCESCA AND PAOLO.

WITHIN the second dolorous circle where
  The lost are whirled, lamenting — thou and I
  Stood, Love, to-day with Dante. Silently
We looked upon the perse and trembling air :
When lo ! from out that darkness of despair
  Two shadows light upon the wind drew nigh,
  So strong the force of the affectionate cry:
And there Francesca, and her lover there.
These when we saw, the wounds whereat they bled,
  Their love which was not with their bodies slain —
These when we saw, great were the tears we shed :
  As, Love, for thee and me love's tears shall rain —
The mortal agony, the nameless dread ;
  The longing, and the passion, and the pain.

XXIX.

THE UNKNOWN WAY.

Two travellers met upon a plain
Where two straight, narrow pathways crossed ;
They met and, with a still surprise,
They looked into each other's eyes
And knew that never, oh, never again !
Could one from the other soul be lost.

But lo ! these narrow pathways lead
Now each from each apart, and lo !
In neither pathway can they go
Together, in their new, strange need.

Far off the purple mountains loom —
Vague and far-off, and fixed as fate —
Which hide from sight that land unknown
Where, ever, like a carven stone
The setting sun doth stand and wait,

And men say not, " Too late ! too late ! "
And sorrow turns to a golden gloom.

But oh, the long journey all unled
By track of traveller o'er the plain —
The stony desert, bleak and rude,
The bruised feet and the tired brain :
And oh, the double solitude,
And oh, the danger and the dread !

XXX.

THE SOWER.

I.

A Sower went forth to sow,
His eyes were wild with woe ;
He crushed the flowers beneath his feet,
Nor smelt the perfume, warm and sweet,
That prayed for pity everywhere.
He came to a field that was harried
By iron, and to heaven laid bare :
He shook the seed that he carried
O'er that brown and bladeless place.
He shook it, as God shakes hail
Over a doomed land,
When lightnings interlace
The sky and the earth, and his wand
Of love is a thunder-flail.

Thus did that Sower sow:
His seed was human blood,
And tears of women and men.
And I, who near him stood,
Said: When the crop comes, then
There will be sobbing and sighing,
Weeping and wailing and crying,
And a woe that is worse than woe.

II.

It was an autumn day
When next I went that way.
And what, think you, did I see?
What was it that I heard?
The song of a sweet-voiced bird?
Nay — but the songs of many,
Thrilled through with praising prayer.
Of all those voices not any
Were sad of memory:
And a sea of sunlight flowed,
And a golden harvest glowed!
On my face I fell down there;

I hid my weeping eyes,
I said : O God, thou art wise !
And I thank thee, again and again,
For the Sower whose name is Pain.

XXXI.

"WHEN THE LAST DOUBT IS DOUBTED."

WHEN the last doubt is doubted,
The last black shadow flown ;
When the last foe is routed,
The last night over and gone :
Then, Love, oh then! there will be rest and peace :
Sweet peace and rest that never thou hast known.

When the hope that in thee moveth
Is born and brought to sight ;
When past is the pain that proveth
The worth of thy new delight :
Oh then, Love! then there will be joy and peace :
Deep peace and joy, bright morning after night.

INTERLUDE.

AS melting snow leaves bare the mountain-side
In spaces that grow wider and more wide,
So melted from the sky the cloudy vail
That hid the face of sun-rise. Land and **ledge**
And waste of glittering waters sent a glare
Back to the smiting sun. The trembling air
Lay, sea on sea, along the horizon's edge ;
And on that upper ocean, clear as glass,
The tall ships followed with deep-mirrored sail
Like clouds wind-moved that follow and that pass ;
And on that upper ocean, far and fair,
Floated the islands all unseen before.
Green grew the ocean shaken through with light,
And blue the heavens flecked with plumy white.

Like pennants on the wind, from o'er the rocks
The birds whirled seaward in shrill-piping flocks :

And through the dawn, as through the shadowy night,
The sound of waves that break upon the shore !

PART IV.

I.

SONG.

LOVE, Love, my Love,
The best things are the truest!
When the earth lies shadowy dark below
Oh then the heavens are bluest!
Deep the blue of the sky,
And sharp the shine of the stars,
And oh, more bright against the night
The Aurora's crimson bars !

THE MIRROR.

THAT I should love thee seemeth meet and wise,
  So beautiful thy beauty he were mad
  Who in thy beauty no deep pleasure had ;
Who felt not the still music of thine eyes
Fall on his forehead, as the evening skies
  The music of the stars feel and are glad.
  But, Love, this thought doth make me wondering
    sad —
Lost in sweet pain of gentle reveries :
That thou shouldst love me is not wise or meet,
  For like thee, Love, I am not beautiful.
    And yet I think that haply in my face
  Thou findest a true beauty — this poor, dull,
Disfigured mirror dimly may repeat
    A little part of thy most heavenly grace.

III.

LIKENESS IN UNLIKENESS.

WE are alike, and yet — oh strange and sweet ! —
　Each in the other difference discerns :
　So the torn strands the maiden's finger turns
Opposing ways, when they again do meet
Clasp each in each, as flame clasps into heat :
　So when my hand on my cool bosom burns,
　Each sense is lost in the other.　So two urns
Upon a shelf the self-same lines repeat ;
But various color gives a lovelier grace,
　And each is finer for its complement.
Thus, Love, it was, I did forget thy face
　As deeper into thy deep soul I went ;
Vague in my mind it grew till, in its place,
　One that I knew not from my own was sent.

IV.

SONG.

NOT from the whole wide world I chose thee —
  Sweetheart, light of the land and the sea!
The wide, wide world could not inclose thee,
  For thou art the whole wide world to me.

ALL IN ONE.

ONCE when a maiden maidenly went by,
  Or when I found some wonder in the grass,
  Or when a purple sunset slow did pass,
Or flaming star fell silent through the sky ;
Once when I heard a singing ecstasy,
  Or saw the moon's face in the river's glass
  Then I remembered that for me, alas !
This beauty must for ever and ever die.
But now I may thus sorrow never more ;
  From fleeting beauty thou hast torn the pall,
For of all beauty, Love, thou art the core,
  And though the empty shadow fading fall, —
Though lesser birds lift up their wings and soar, —
  In having thee alone, Love, I have all.

VI.

"I COUNT MY TIME BY TIMES THAT I MEET THEE."

I COUNT my time by times that I meet thee ;
  These are my yesterdays, my morrows, noons
  And nights ; these my old moons and my new
    moons.
Slow fly the hours, fast the hours flee,
If thou art far from or art near to me :
  If thou art far, the birds' tunes are no tunes ;
  If thou art near, the wintry days are Junes, —
Darkness is light, and sorrow cannot be.
Thou art my dream come true, and thou my dream,
  The air I breathe, the world wherein I dwell ;
    My journey's end thou art, and thou the way ;
Thou art what I would be, yet only seem ;
  Thou art my heaven and thou art my hell ;
    Thou art my ever-living judgment day.

VII.

SONG.

YEARS have flown since I knew thee first,
And I know thee as water is known of thirst:
Yet I knew thee of old at the first sweet sight,
And thou art strange to me, Love, to-night.

VIII.

THE SEASONS.

O STRANGE Spring days, when from the shivering
    ground
Love riseth, wakening from his dreamful swound
And, frightened, in the stream his face hath found !

O Summer days, when Love hath grown apace,
And feareth not to look upon Love's face,
And lightnings burn where earth and sky embrace !

O Autumn, when the winds are dank and dread,
How brave above the dying and the dead
The conqueror, Love, uplifts his banner red !

O Winter, when the earth lies white and chill !
Now only hath strong Love his perfect will
Whom heat, nor cold, nor death can bind or kill.

IX.

"SUMMER'S RAIN AND WINTER'S SNOW."

Summer's rain and winter's snow
With the seasons come and go ;
   Shine and shower ;
Tender bud and perfect flower ;
Silver blossom, golden fruit ;
   Song and lute,
With their inward sound of pain :
Winter's snow and summer's rain ;
   Frost and fire ;
Joy beyond the heart's desire, —
And our June comes round again.

X.

THE VIOLIN.

BEFORE the listening world here bold I stand,
　The hot air quivers with my passionate play ;
　I hear their clappings, and their feet alway
Follow with storm some passage glad or grand :
And now they fall to weeping at my hand,
　And now they hear the trump of judgment day,
　And now one white small note to heaven doth stray
And fluttering fall upon the golden sand.
But like the murmur of the distant sea
　Their loud applause, and far, oh, far and weak
Soundeth my own strong music unto me —
　Far from the soul of music that doth speak
In wordless wail and joyful agony
　From this dear thing I press against my cheek.

XI.

"MY SONGS ARE ALL OF THEE."

My songs are all of thee, what though I sing
  Of morning when the stars are yet in sight,
  Of evening, or the melancholy night,
Of birds that o'er the reddening waters wing ;
Of song, of fire, of winds, or mists that cling
  To mountain-tops, of winter all in white,
  Of rivers that toward ocean take their flight,
Of summer when the rose is blossoming.
I think no thought that is not thine, no breath
  Of life I breathe beyond thy sanctity ;
Thou art the voice that silence uttereth,
  And of all sound thou art the sense. Of thee
Is my song's music, and what my song saith
  Is but the beat of thy heart, throbbed through me.

XII.

WEAL AND WOE.

O HIGHEST, strongest, sweetest woman-soul !
   Thou holdest in the compass of thy grace
   All the strange fate and passion of thy race ;
Of the old, primal curse thou knowest the whole :
Thine eyes, too wise, are heavy with the dole,
   The doubt, the dread of all this human maze ;
   Thou in the virgin morning of thy days
Hast felt the bitter waters o'er thee roll.
Yet thou knowest, too, the terrible delight,
   The still content, the solemn ecstasy ;
     Whatever sharp, sweet bliss thy kind may know.
    Thy spirit is deep for pleasure as for woe —
   Deep as the rich, dark-caverned, awful sea
That the keen-winded, glimmering dawn makes white.

XIII.

"OH, LOVE IS NOT A SUMMER MOOD."

I.

OH, LOVE is not a summer mood,
   Nor flying phantom of the brain,
Nor youthful fever of the blood,
      Nor dream, nor fate, nor circumstance.
      Love is not born of blinded chance,
      Nor bred in simple ignorance.

II.

But love hath winter in her blood,
   And love is fruit of holy pain,
And perfect flower of maidenhood.
      True love is steadfast as the skies,
      And once alight she never flies;
      And love is strong, and still, and wise.

7

XIV.

"LOVE IS NOT BOND TO ANY MAN."

I.

Love is not bond to any man,
  Nor slave of woman, howso fair.
Love knows no architect or plan :
        She is a lawless wanderer,
        She hath no master over her,
        And worships not her worshipper.

II.

But though she knoweth law nor plan —
  Though she is free as light and air —
Love was a slave since time began.
        Lo, now, behold a wondrous thing :
        Love may be led by silken string,
        Yet from stone walls she taketh wing.

XV.

SONG.

HE knows not the path of duty
  Who says that the way is sweet;
But he who is blind to the beauty,
  And finds but thorns for his feet.

He alone is the perfect giver
  Who swears that his gift is naught;
And he is the sure receiver
  Who gains what he never sought.

Against the darkness outer
  God's light his likeness takes,
And he from the mighty doubter
  The great believer makes.

Like the pale, cold moon above her
  With its heart of the heart of fire,
My Love is the one true lover,
  And hers is the soul of desire.

AFTER-SONG.

AFTER-SONG.

THROUGH love to light! Oh wonderful the way
    That leads from darkness to the perfect day!
From darkness and from dolor of the night
To morning that comes singing o'er the sea.
Through love to light! Through light, O God, to
      thee,
Who art the love of love, the eternal light of light!

CONTENTS.

CONTENTS.

——◆——

PART III.

CONTENTS.   III

PART IV.

₊ The Decorations of this volume were engraved by Mr Henry Marsh.